Say Hello to the Buffalo

Say Hello to the Buffalo

MILES GIBSON

Illustrated by Chris Riddell

Heinemann · London

First published in Great Britain 1994
by Heinemann Young Books
an imprint of Reed Consumer Books Limited
Michelin House, 81 Fulham Road, London SW3 6RB
and Auckland, Melbourne, Singapore and Toronto

ISBN 0 434 97557 5

A CIP catalogue record for this book is
available at the British Library

Printed by
St. Edmundsbury Press, Bury St. Edmunds, Suffolk

Contents

Stick Insects	7
Fox	8
Bats	9
Leopard	10
Germs	12
Worm	13
Hyenas	14
Pig	16
Pangolin	17
Birds	18
Lions	19
Hamster	20
Frogs	21
Buffalo	22
Porcupine	24
Mice	27
Goat	28
Python	30
Cats	31
Spider	32

Dodo	34
Bear	35
Hippopotamus	36
Giraffe	38
Pike	40
Chickens	41
Beetles	42
Dog	43
Dragon	44
Shark	46
Rat	48
Snail	49
Elephant	50
Crabs	52
Pigeon	54
Quagga	55
Tiger	56
Dromedary	58
Gannet	59
Animal Alphabet	60

Stick Insects

Dogs bite
Cats scratch
Parrots swear like brickies
Mice smell bad
Rabbits kick
Fish are dismal thickies

So Jason bought himself a box
Of Phasma – baby stickies

A sticky is quite interesting
And can grow fairly big
But spends an awful lot of time
Looking like a twig

Jason tried to talk to them
And teach them simple tricks
But they never got beyond
Imitating sticks

Fox

The fox it has to be confessed
Has one unpleasant habit
He can't resist the pleasures
Of dining on the rabbit
And the chicken and the duckling
And the pheasant and the grouse
And the moorhen and the gosling
And the squirrel and the mouse
In every other manner
He's the perfect country gent
From his Burberry and gaiters
To his monocle and scent
But like the aristocracy
His only claims to fame
Are skills in making enemies
And taste for seasoned game

Bats

Alice liked to levitate
Despite the strictest warning
Endeavouring to roost with bats
From dusk till early morning
By hanging from the rafters
On the whisker of a thread
Until she fell asleep up there
And falling, cracked her head

Leopard

The leopard is the sort of cat
You shouldn't keep inside a flat
Because he suffers deprivation
Held for long in captivation

He's happiest when running free
Or sleeping in a sun-baked tree
He doesn't care to be restrained
And never can be toilet trained

So don't ignore this good advice
Unless you want to pay the price
For keeping his bad temper sweet
By risking both your hands and feet

A leopard when he's aggravated
Grows extremely animated
Piddles on the chairs and beds
And rips the furnishings to shreds

Germs

The germ is smaller than a speck
And quite impossible to check
They enter through the kitchen drain
For reasons no one can explain
Ten thousand lodge inside your nose
And thousands more between your toes
They cover you as soft as rain
And give you fever on the brain
They try to make you sweat and freeze
Until you shiver, cough and sneeze
Since germs know every nasty trick
It's not surprising you feel sick

Worm

The worm is cautious even shy
Yet makes a faithful friend
Unless you should insult him by
Addressing his wrong end

Hyenas

Hyenas laugh until they choke
But never want to share the joke

It's thought to be contrarious
To find life so hilarious
While forced to eat abandoned bones
With jaws equipped for cracking stones

Whatever causes their good mood
It can't be the disgusting food

Pig

Although the porker may look grim
He's really rather neat and prim
By nature but requires assistance
Keeping mud at some safe distance
From his soft and snuffling snout
And splashing all his friends about
Him when by chance he grows demented
By the smell of sweet fermented
Apples rotting under trees
For though the mud may reach his knees
He'll plunge about and think it fine
To act like any common swine
If only pigs wore wooden clogs
They'd smell a little less like hogs

Pangolin

A pangolin wears armour plate
It's something he would advocate
To all who feed on crawly things
It helps prevent the painful stings
Of termites, ants and all the rest
When lunch is taken in their nest

Birds

Penguins favour names like Clancy
Theodore, Hubert and Nancy
Common gulls are often plain
Gary, Tracy, Scott or Wayne
Puffins on the other hand
Try to sound immensely grand
Lavender and Tristram Shandy
Are two names that come in handy

NB: The Albatross – if you're a tripper
Must always be addressed as Skipper

Lions

Lions eat vegetarians
They swipe 'em with a paw
They like to know each one is fresh
Because they eat 'em raw

Hamster

The hamster makes a horrid smell
There's nothing else he does so well
As causing that peculiar stink
To make the bravest person shrink
Away from the endurance test
Of cleaning out a hamster's nest
The reason hamsters smell like drains
Has baffled all the finest brains
Unless of course and who can tell
The hamster likes that horrid smell

Frogs

Frogs may come in different shades
And several useful sizes
You grow them in the garden pool
Or places where it's damp and cool
They love to enter pet parades
But seldom win top prizes

Toads in contrast to the frogs
Have few redeeming graces
Sulking is their chief vocation
Belching without provocation
They startle unsuspecting dogs
And pull revolting faces

Buffalo

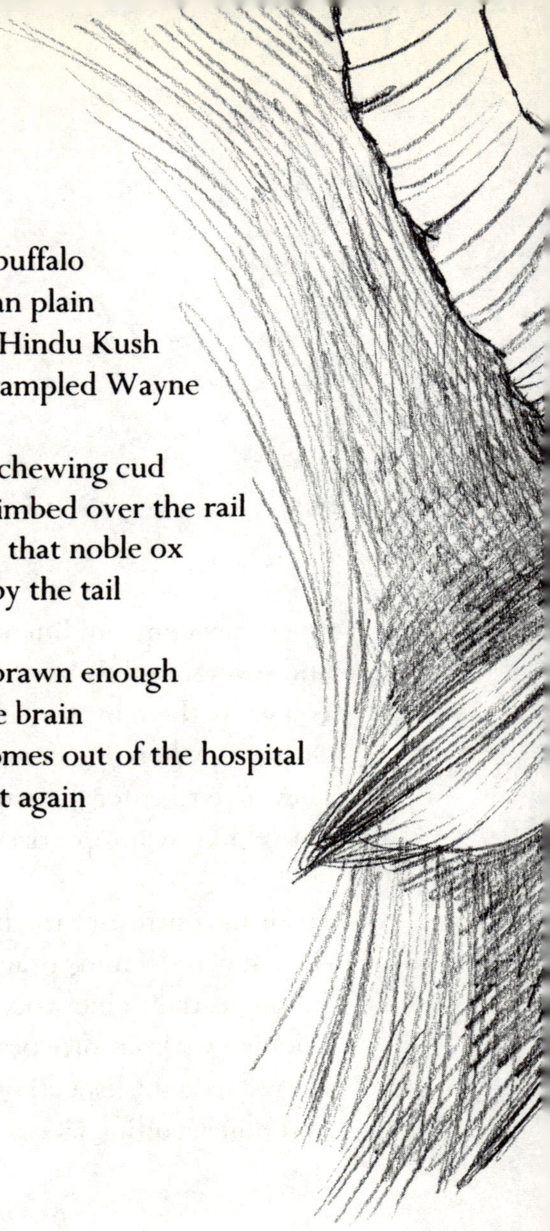

Say hello to the buffalo
Lord of the Indian plain
Bully boy of the Hindu Kush
The beast that trampled Wayne

The buffalo was chewing cud
When Wayne climbed over the rail
Swaggered up to that noble ox
And shook him by the tail

The buffalo has brawn enough
But a very simple brain
When Wayne comes out of the hospital
He won't try that again

Porcupine

The porcupine has few good friends
If you exclude his brothers
His shambling skirt of dusty quills
Prevents him learning social skills
And as you know so much depends
On mixing well with others

His conversation is so poor
It's something like a snuffle
An insult to the cockatoo
Or educated kangaroo
And when the dancers take the floor
His waltz is just a shuffle

He shirks the social gathering
Ignores all invitations
The very thought of getting dressed
Makes any porcupine depressed
He loathes the witless blathering
Detests the irritations

He much prefers his fireside chair
He cares not for rejection
With pork pie and a pickled egg
And home made beer drawn from the keg
He'll sit at home without a care
Content with introspection

Mice

Mice have a taste for bacon rind
Porridge oats and kippers
Remember this if you should find
Mice nesting in your slippers

Goat

The goat – a sort of sheep with horns
Must live on thistles, roots and thorns
Which might explain his fractious bouts
Of chasing brownies and boy scouts
And biting buckles from the shoes
Of whomsoever he may choose

While those inclined to make a fuss
Will never have it answered thus
Understand
It's just a question
Of his chronic indigestion

Python

A python can be charming
With his smiling polished face
But always treat with caution
His cunning slow embrace
When it starts above your elbows
And works towards your feet
He's probably attached to you
Because you taste so sweet

Cats

It's said that cats have magic powers
Because they talk to stones and flowers
And stalk the ghosts and midnight elves
That dwell among the kitchen shelves
Despite the rumours of black magic
The truth, alas, is frankly tragic
For though they look extremely wise
It should not fill you with surprise
To learn that cats are rather dense
Possessing little common sense
Since cats have brains the size of peas
They're scarcely smarter than their fleas

Spider

Geraldine loved a spider
That she found beneath a rug
She called him Mr Harris
And she kept him in a jug

A hairy sort of spider
With several staring eyes
And a rather nasty habit
Of eating captured flies

Geraldine loved a spider
But the end was very grim
Someone filled the jug with milk
Poor Harris could not swim

Geraldine blames her mother
And her mother blames her dad
They're sorry for the accident
But the flies are very glad

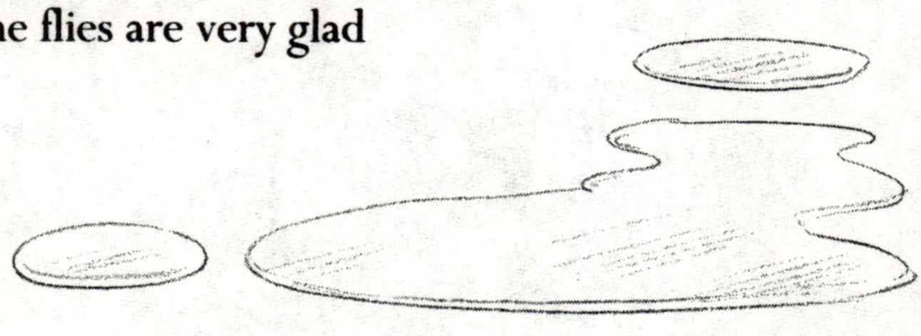

Dodo

The dodo suffered extinction
Failing to make the distinction
Between ornithologists with books
And common sailors with hungry looks

The bear – a most notorious glutton
Loved nothing more than boiled mutton
Served with fried eggs, toast and beans
Tomatoes, onions, boiled greens
His mother – quite a portly bruin
Denied she'd led her son to ruin
Although the doctors all agree
That after such a thunderous tea
It was the ice cream à la mode
That made the tragic bear explode

Hippopotamus

There is always such a lotamus
Of the friendly hippopotamus
Sandra bruised her knees
Knocked down by a hippolotamus sneeze

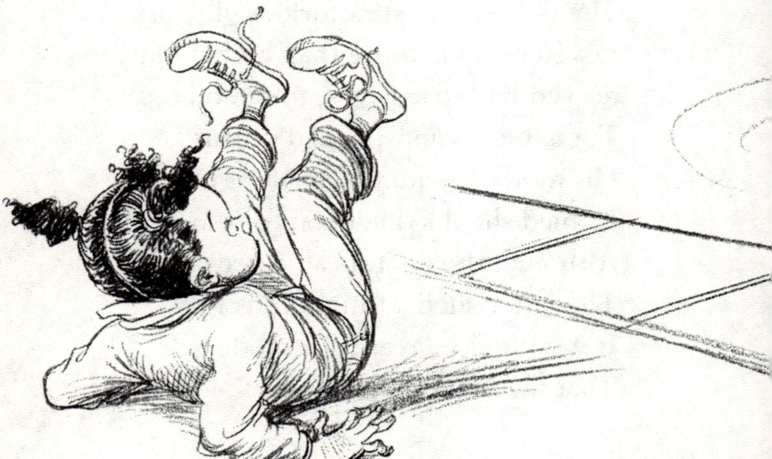

Giraffe

You'll find that the giraffe
Is far too proud
To engage in conversation
He'll stand with his head
Tipped into the cloud
Ignoring your salutation
He's never been known
To grant interviews
And shuns private consultation
For he likes to pretend
He is lost to the world
In some lofty contemplation

He has yet to master the alphabet
If that's any consolation

Pike

A pike will snatch at anything
That wriggles past his snout
He's a pirate of the bulrush bed
A bruiser and a lout

A pike will snap up tiddlers
And just to chance his luck
He'll sink his teeth into the feet
Of moorhen, coot and duck

He'll try to bite your sandals
But he much prefers to wait
For tiny unprotected toes
Such appetising bait

We shouldn't persecute the pike
For those in crime prevention
Insist that with each beastly act
He cries out for attention

Chickens

Chickens have to live on shelves
In giant factory sheds
So it isn't such a great surprise
When they go off their heads

Beetles

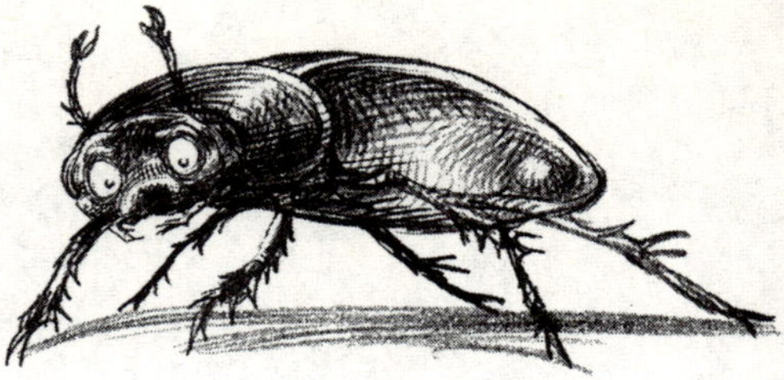

Janice likes eating beetles
The crunchy sort are the best
She also likes eating gravel
But it's difficult to digest

Janice likes eating beetles
Of every size and shape
She once tried to feed her brother
But her brother made his escape

Janice likes eating beetles
The doctor sent her to bed
Janice enjoys her punishment
Now she's eating feathers instead

Dog

Arnold was given a little dog
By his barmy old Uncle Blake
(Although Arnold had asked for a poisonous frog
from a distant African lake)

Arnold sulked and refused to keep
The poor unfortunate pet
So Arnold was finally put to sleep
By a sympathetic vet

Dragon

There's a dragon in the garden
Asleep in the potting shed
He's as knobbly as a crocodile
But he has no teeth in his poor old head

He lives on sweet milk puddings
With sponge cakes soaked in wine
And sometimes takes a sandwich
If you cut it very fine

He says he came from China
In the days when his skin was gold
But his screws are loose and he talks in his sleep
It's sad to be so old

POT

Shark

The shark – as you know – is misunderstood
He'll eat anything, but he would if he could
Dine only on winkles and oysters and such
The kind of small fry that don't mind very much
If they find themselves in the throat of a shark
Where it's dreadfully hot and fearfully dark

But the shark has a ponderous appetite
So he can't stop himself when taking a bite
From children in swimsuits and old men in boats
And anything else that paddles or floats
He hates to be such a bloodthirsty sinner
It's terribly hard when they all smell like dinner

Rat

Frank had a rat who had grown so fat
That he even frightened the neighbour's cat
They lived in a very cold basement flat
And the rat had to sleep in his coat and hat

Snail

The snail makes a most acceptable pet
If you're fond of the ornamental
But sulks in its shell for days at a time
And is prone to be temperamental

The social life of these gastropods
Is the subject of some speculation
They are seen to slobber and cling to their friends
In perpetual lamentation

Elephant

Always be kind to your elephant
Resist the sarcastic remark
About the size of his stomach
And his morbid dread of the dark

The elephant is a sensitive beast
So any improper suggestion
Can swiftly shatter his confidence
And ruin his fragile digestion

Crabs

Crabs are very curious
And have their eyes on stalks
For when the tide is low enough
They go for bracing walks

To gather in the sand dunes
Where sometimes late at night
You can hear them singing shanties
And clacking with delight

Because the ocean is so cold
And life down there is drab
Such interludes upon the beach
Are loved by every crab

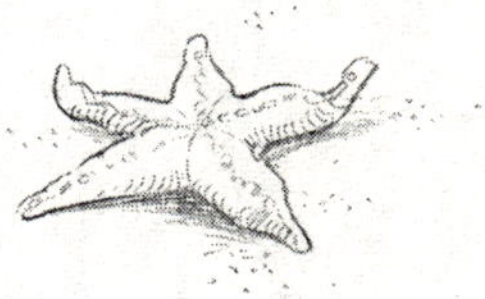

It's the perfect social evening
Where famous crabs parade
In a festival of music
And a crusty masquerade

Pigeon

If God gave the pigeon a hand
It would save him blunting his beak
He'd wear gloves of a most superior brand
And carry a flask when the weather was bleak

If God gave the pigeon a hand
He could lift his head from the gutter
And be welcome to dine anywhere in the Strand
Where they always serve breadcrumbs with butt

Quagga

The quagga is an animal
You won't see in the zoo
Not a zebra nor an ass
But a mixture of the two
He lived in Southern Africa
Without regret or dread
When hunters stumbled over him
And promptly shot him dead
Now the quagga is extinct
And you'll never see his tracks
He disappeared entirely
To make little leather sacks

Tiger

Thelma's mother Lady Pond
Is very fond of cats
Judging by the wardrobe full
Of leopard gloves and hats

The tiger skin upon her back
Makes other mothers gloat
Since they cannot afford to wear
This most impressive coat

Thelma isn't very pleased
And tells her mother that
A tiger skin looks at its best
While still upon the cat

Thelma's mother scolds the child
For wanting to deprive
Her of the coat that gives a roar
And swallows her alive

Dromedary

It requires an apothecary
To treat the dromedary
For the poisonous halitosis
At the root of his neurosis

A bottle of tonic
Or full strength pulmonic
As a cure for distemper
Might sweeten his temper

Gannet

Of all the birds upon the planet
No one loves the thieving gannet

He bullies other birds and begs
A chance to steal and eat their eggs

He plots his air supremacy
With undisguised contumacy

He's also guilty of some crimes
For which there are no ready rimes

Be satisfied with this advice
Avoid the bird at any price

Animal Alphabet

A is for Aardvark
Very welcome grilled
B is for Bat
Best when eaten chilled
C is for Crocodile
Foamy green milk shakes
D is for Donkey
Good with griddle cakes
E is for Emu
Gently poached in wine
F is for Ferret
Softly steeped in brine
G is for Gorilla
Boiled and thinly sliced

H is for Hyena
Tempting chopped or diced
I is for Iguana
The perfect Sunday roast
J is for Jackal
Spread on buttered toast
K is for Kangaroo
Very lightly braised
L is for Leopard
A flavour greatly praised

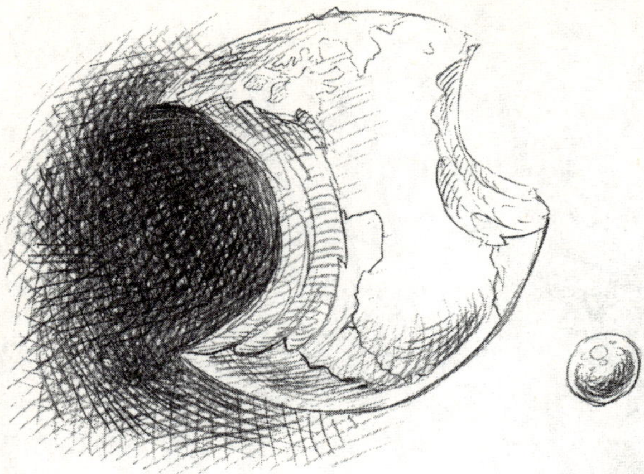

M is for Monkey
Cutlets quickly fried
N is for Natterjack
Pickled, spiced or dried
O is for Otter
Always served with rice
P is for Porcupine
A taste like crunchy mice
Q is for Quail
Tumbled in a skillet
R is for Rhinoceros
Famous for the fillet
S is for Squirrel
With bacon and carrot

T is for Tortoise
With sage sauce and parrot
U is for Umpteen
Different tasty fowl
V is for Vulture
Cold with curried owl
W is for Whale
But it's too late for him
X marks the spot
Where the Whale used to swim
Y is for Yak
A favourite at feasts
Z is for Zebra
The tenderest of beasts

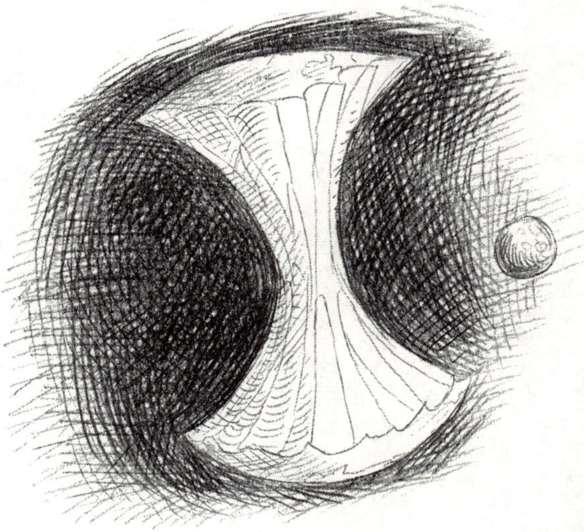